THE
GERMAN
SHEPHERD

by Charlotte Wilcox

C A P S T O N E   P R E S S
M A N K A T O ,   M I N N E S O T A

C A P S T O N E   P R E S S
818 North Willow Street • Mankato, MN 56001

Printed in the United States of America.

Library of Congress Cataloging-in-Publication Data
Wilcox, Charlotte.
    The German shepherd/by Charlotte Wilcox
    p. cm.
    Includes bibliographical references (p. 45) and index.
    Summary: An introduction to this intelligent, fearless dog, which includes its history, development, uses, and care.
    ISBN 1-56065-398-1
    1. German shepherd dogs--Juvenile literature. [1. German shepherd dogs.] I. Title. II. Series: Wilcox, Charlotte. Learning about dogs.
SF429.G37W535 1996
636.7'37--dc20

                                                    96-26568
                                                      CIP
                                                       AC

Photo credits
Unicorn, cover; Marie Mills, 12, 34; Fred Johnson, 16;
        Dick Young, 24; Gary L. Johnson, 30.
Archive Photos, 6, 20.
Reynolds Photography, 8, 10, 36, 38-39, 40.
FPG, 14, 18, 22, 28.
Kelly Gaylor, 26.
Cheryl Blair, 32.

Table of Contents

Words in **boldface** type in the text are defined
in the Glossary in the back of this book.

Quick Facts about the German Shepherd

Description

Height:
: Males stand 24 to 26 inches (61 to 66 centimeters) and females stand 22 to 24 inches (56 to 61 centimeters) from the ground to the top of the shoulders.

Weight:
: German shepherds weigh 55 to 95 pounds (25 to 43 kilograms). Males weigh a little more than females.

Physical features:
: German shepherds have long, sturdy bodies built for strength and endurance. Their heads have long muzzles, pointed ears, black noses, and dark, almond-shaped eyes. Their tails are long and thick.

Color:
: German shepherds can have black areas on their bodies, heads, and tails. The rest of their coat is a shade of yellow, tan, brown, or gray. Some are all black. They can also be white.

4

Development

Place of origin: German shepherds originated in Germany.

History of breed: German shepherds descended from herding dogs bred by a German army captain in the late 1800s.

Numbers: Almost 80,000 German shepherds are **registered** each year in the United States, plus about 8,500 in Canada. Many more are born every year but are not registered.

Uses

German shepherds work in law enforcement, search and rescue, and as **guide dogs** or **service dogs** for persons with disabilities. Many German shepherds are family pets or farm dogs.

Chapter 1

Companion and Protector

German shepherds are one of the most popular dog breeds in North America. They are intelligent. They are loyal and devoted to their owners. They are fearless. Their appearance is rugged, and they are known to be fierce watchdogs. But they are very loving with their owners. German shepherds are the perfect mix of companion and protector.

German shepherds are the most popular dog with police forces. Because they are smart and

German shepherds look fierce, but they are very loving with their owners.

fearless, they are often heroes. German shepherds have an excellent sense of smell. In Denmark and Holland, German shepherds are trained to find gas leaks. They have been known to find breaks in gas pipes buried under highways. A German shepherd was also the first guide dog for the blind.

One of the most famous German shepherds was Rin Tin Tin. He starred in his first movie in 1923. The first Rin Tin Tin made more than 40 movies in his nine-year career. He earned $1 million. Since then, other dogs named Rin Tin Tin have carried on the story in television and books.

German shepherds are smart and alert. They can be trained to do many things.

Chapter 2

Beginnings of the German Shepherd

For centuries, farmers have used dogs to herd animals. Their dogs had a natural instinct to circle prey and look for strays. This made it easy to train them to herd. People tried to breed dogs with the best qualities for herding.

Farmers needed dogs big enough to control their animals and fast enough to keep up with them. They had to be gentle enough not to hurt the animals. They needed good eyes and ears to guard against wolves or thieves. They needed courage to protect the farmer and his livestock.

German shepherds have very good senses.

Germans shepherds were first trained to herd animals.

Farmers bred dogs that were suited to the needs of their region. In colder climates, the dogs had thicker coats. In mountain areas, dogs had strong legs for climbing. They developed special talents depending on whether they herded sheep, cattle, or goats. Many sizes, colors, and types of herding dogs began to appear.

The Sheepdogs of Europe

Early Europeans raised sturdy herding dogs of various colors and shapes. Some of these ancient breeds survive today as **sheepdogs** in Belgium, France, Holland, and Great Britain.

People in Germany were especially proud of their herding dogs. German farmers learned to breed dogs to get the qualities they wanted. People in each region had definite ideas about how their dogs should look and act.

Over the years, German farmers developed dogs that were not only good at their jobs, but were symbols of their region. Farmers bred their dogs to produce puppies of the color and type popular in their region. Dogs from each region had a unique appearance that set them apart from those of other regions.

One of these unique, talented breeds later became the German shepherd. It started with the birth of one puppy.

German shepherds are usually black and tan.

The New Year's Puppy

On New Year's Day, 1895, a German farm dog gave birth to a litter of puppies. They looked like many of the shepherd dogs from central Germany. They were black and tan and had dark eyes and noses. Their large paws and deep chests showed that they would grow to be strong and able shepherds.

One of the puppies soon showed the intelligence and personality of a good working dog. He was a fearless explorer. He guarded his family when strangers visited. He chased anything that moved.

But the puppy's owner did not train him. Soon, his curious mind got him into trouble. With no training and no work to do, the puppy found ways to keep from being bored. He was always knocking something over or chasing another animal. He would even pick fights with other dogs. He was on his way to becoming a problem dog.

A Captain to the Rescue

One day, a German army captain spotted this rowdy dog. The captain saw more than just trouble. He saw a future champion. Captain Max von Stephanitz was a great dog lover. He wanted to breed the perfect shepherd dog. And he knew a good one when he saw it. The captain took the young dog home and named him Horand.

The captain immediately began obedience training. Horand learned quickly. Soon, he was well behaved and able to perform many useful duties. Horand became the pride of the captain's home. He had perfect manners around friends and children. And he was the perfect guard against unwanted strangers.

The Father of a Breed

Captain von Stephanitz saw a lot more in Horand than just a good working dog. He saw the father of a breed. The captain was right. Horand passed his qualities on to his offspring.

In 1899, the captain started the German Shepherd Dog Club. The club set up standards for how German shepherds should look and what qualities they should have. Horand was the perfect example of these standards.

A German shepherd is a good working dog. Some are trained to be police dogs.

Chapter 3

Development of the German Shepherd

At first, only Horand, his offspring, and a few other similar-looking dogs were allowed to be registered with the new German Shepherd Dog Club. Later, other top herding dogs were crossed into the breed.

The first German shepherd came to North America about 1908. The German Shepherd Dog Club of America began five years later. By the end of World War II (1939-1945), the German shepherd was famous around the world. Horand's offspring lived and worked in almost every country on earth.

German shepherds were trained to serve in wars.

War Heroes

The German army was the first to train dogs for use in war. German shepherds had all the qualities the army wanted. In the early 1900s, the German government encouraged its people to raise German shepherds. It set up clubs in villages to train the dogs for military and rescue work.

When World War I started in 1914, Germany had 6,000 trained dogs ready to go to war. In all, 20,000 dogs fought for Germany in World War I. They carried messages across battlefields, brought medicine to wounded soldiers, patrolled borders, and stood guard duty.

During four years of fighting, soldiers from many countries saw these dogs in action. Germany and its allies lost the war, but their dogs were winners. German shepherds were soon admired by army people around the world.

German shepherds are used for search and rescue.

German shepherds were used in war. They even had to wear gas masks to breathe.

After the war, the conquering armies kept some of their people in Germany. Soldiers from the United States, Canada, England, and other countries met German shepherds up close. They adopted German shepherds and brought them home. The German shepherd soon won the hearts of families throughout Europe and North America. By 1925, German shepherds

Chapter 5

The German Shepherd in Action

Of all the German shepherd's qualities, one that sets it apart is its intelligence. German shepherds are among the smartest of all breeds. This keeps them at the top of the list for police work and for helping persons with disabilities. Only the smartest, most talented dogs can succeed at these jobs.

Dogs in Law Enforcement

Until recently, almost all police dogs were German shepherds. They are still the favorites of many police officers. German shepherds work with police in almost every country of the world.

Police dogs do things that human officers cannot do. They can smell drugs, guns, or bombs

The German shepherd is one of the smartest dog breeds.

German shepherds are part of many police departments.

hidden in buildings and vehicles. They can trail
the scent of a lost person or an escaped prisoner
for miles. They can hear sounds humans cannot
hear. They can crawl through small spaces where
people cannot go.

Dogs can find their way in the dark better than
people can. They can run faster and jump higher.
Dogs can find and catch criminal suspects even if
they hide. They will only bark at a suspect who

stands still and waits for the officer, but they will attack one who tries to run away.

A Dog Named Dox

One of the most talented police dogs of all time was a German shepherd named Dox. He could untie knots and unload a gun. He even kept a child from being hit by a car.

Once, Dox cornered 12 criminals all by himself. He kept them standing with their arms raised until police officers arrived and arrested them. One criminal escaped from Dox, but the dog remembered him. He nabbed the criminal the next time he saw him, six years later.

Another time, Dox chased a burglar running from a crime scene. The burglar shot Dox in the leg. With a shattered leg, Dox kept going and brought the burglar down. By the time Dox was 14, he had been shot seven times. He recovered from every bullet.

Guide Dogs and More

As people saw the amazing things police dogs could do, the idea of using dogs to help blind

people took shape. The first guide dogs for the blind were trained in Europe during the 1920s. Guide dogs lead blind people through streets and buildings. They help them avoid traffic and running into things.

In 1927, a blind teenager heard about a guide-dog program called The Seeing Eye. His name was Morris Frank. Frank's dream of having a guide dog came true. Frank traveled to Switzerland to meet a female German shepherd named Buddy. After weeks of training, Frank and Buddy went home to Tennessee. Buddy was the first Seeing Eye dog in North America.

German shepherds also make good **signal dogs** for deaf people. They alert their owners to sounds like doorbells, clocks, or fire alarms. Some German shepherds work as service dogs for disabled people. They open and close doors, carry things, and turn lights on and off.

A German shepherd was the first seeing eye dog. They are often the dog of choice for the blind.

Chapter 6

A German Shepherd of Your Own

German shepherds make good family pets as long as they have plenty of activity and do not get bored. They need attention, affection, exercise, and firm discipline. An adult must be in control of a German shepherd at all times.

Where to Get a German Shepherd

If you are interested in buying a dog, the German Shepherd Dog Club in your area is a good place to start looking. Or ask a **veterinarian** to direct you to a breeder. Breeders sell puppies and often have older dogs for sale, too.

Another place to find a German shepherd is at a rescue shelter for orphaned animals. The shelter makes sure the dogs are healthy and safe. You may not find a purebred German shepherd at a

German shepherds need plenty of activity, and they love to be outdoors.

To be a purebred German shepherd, both dog's parents must be registered.

shelter. Breeders keep **pedigrees** of their dogs and can assure you that a dog is purebred.

Keeping a German Shepherd

A German shepherd needs to be with people. It should not be left alone day after day. It should only be tied up for short periods of time. The dog should have a corner in your house where it eats and sleeps. Provide a food dish, a water dish, and a dog bed or cage with a blanket.

German shepherds need at least two hours of exercise every day. If you have a yard with a dog-proof fence, the dog can play outside. You will also need to take it for a walk every day. If you do not have a yard, take the dog for longer walks.

Every German shepherd can benefit from obedience training. If your dog is not already trained, start the training right away. Even older dogs can be trained.

To protect your dog from being lost or stolen, have your name and telephone number engraved on the collar. Or have a veterinarian implant a microchip under its skin. A microchip is a computer chip about the size of a grain of rice. When scanned, it will tell the owner's name, address, and telephone number.

Your Dog's Diet

A full-grown German shepherd may eat one to two pounds (up to one kilogram) of dry or semimoist dog food, or two to three cans of canned food every day. The amount depends on the dog's size, age, and how much work it does. Feed the dog once a day or divide the food into two meals. Feed the dog at the same time and in

Withers

Hindquarters

Hock

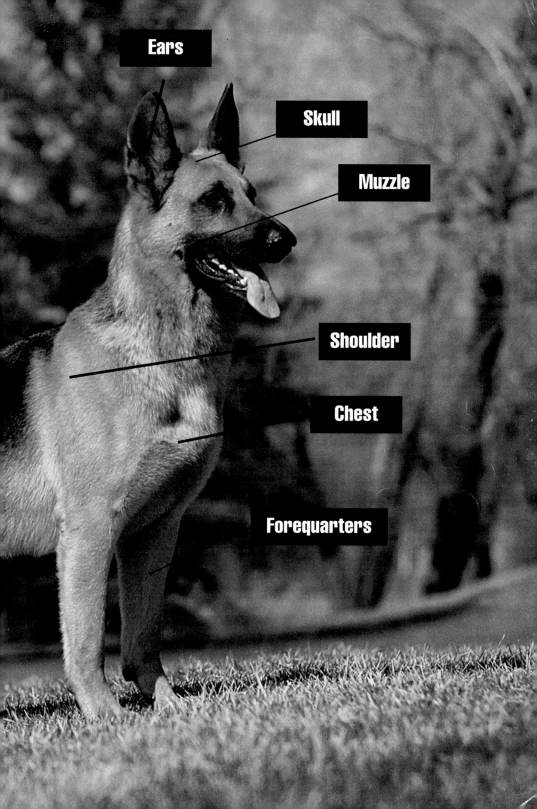

Ears

Skull

Muzzle

Shoulder

Chest

Forequarters

A police dog can be an officer's best friend.

the same place every day. Keep fresh water out all the time or make sure your dog drinks at least three times a day.

Grooming

German shepherds shed a lot, especially in the spring. Brush the dog to remove shedding hairs. Puppies should never have baths, but a grown dog can have a bath once or twice a year as needed.

Give your dog a rawhide bone to chew to help clean its teeth. Clean the teeth with a wet cloth or brush them with a dog toothbrush and toothpaste. Trim the dog's nails if they get too long. Take the dog to a veterinarian or professional groomer if you have never trimmed a dog's nails before.

A Healthy Pet

Dogs need shots every year to protect them from serious diseases that can kill them and spread to humans. They also need pills to protect them from **heartworms**.

During warm weather, check for ticks. Some ticks carry **Lyme disease**, which can cripple a dog or human. Put rubbing alcohol on the tick and pull it out with tweezers. Drown it in the alcohol or bleach. Check often for fleas, lice, and mites. Special sprays and shampoos can get rid of them.

Even though they are famous as police and guide dogs, most German shepherds never have that kind of job. Most are family dogs. And loving a family is the job German shepherds probably like best.

Quick Facts about Dogs

Dog Terms

A male is simply called a dog. A female dog is called a bitch. A young dog is a puppy until it is one year old. A newborn puppy is a whelp until it is **weaned**. A family of puppies born at one time is called a litter.

Life History

Origin: All dogs, wolves, coyotes, and **dingoes** descended from a single wolflike dog. Dogs have been friends of humans since earliest times.

Types: There are many colors, shapes, and sizes of dogs. Full-grown dogs weigh from two pounds (one kilogram) to more than 200 pounds (90 kilograms). They are from six inches (15 centimeters) to three feet (90 centimeters) tall. They can have thick hair or almost no hair, long or short legs, and many types of ears, faces, and tails. There are about 350 different dog breeds in the world.

Reproductive life: Dogs mature at six to 18 months. Puppies are born two months after breeding. A female can have two litters per year. An average litter is three to six puppies, but litters of 15 or more are possible.

Development: Puppies are born blind and deaf. Their ears and eyes open at one to two weeks. They try to walk at about two weeks. At three weeks, their teeth begin to come in, and they are ready to start weaning.

| Life span: | Dogs are fully grown at two years. If well cared for, they may live about 15 years. |

The Dog's Super Senses

Smell:	Dogs have a sense of smell many times stronger than a human's. Dogs use their supersensitive noses even more than their eyes and ears. They recognize people, animals, and objects just by smelling them, sometimes from long distances away or for days afterward.
Hearing:	Dogs hear far better than humans. Not only can dogs hear things from farther away, they can hear high-pitched sounds people cannot.
Sight:	Dogs are **color-blind**. Some scientists think dogs can tell some colors. Others think dogs see everything in black and white. Dogs can see twice as wide around them as humans can because their eyes are on the sides of their heads.
Touch:	Dogs enjoy being petted more than almost any other animal. They can feel vibrations like an approaching train or an earthquake soon to happen.
Taste:	Dogs do not taste much. This is partly because their sense of smell is so strong that it overpowers the taste. It is also partly because they swallow their food too quickly to taste it well.
Navigation:	Dogs can often find their way through crowded streets or across miles of wilderness without any guidance. This is a special dog sense that scientists do not fully understand.

Glossary

color-blind—unable to see colors or the difference between colors

dingo—wild Australian dogs

guide dog—a dog trained to lead a blind person

heartworm—tiny worm carried by mosquitoes that enters a dog's heart and slowly destroys it

Lyme disease—a disease carried by ticks that causes illness, pain, and sometimes paralysis in animals and humans

muzzle—the part of a dog's head that is in front of the eyes, including the nose and mouth

offspring—sons and daughters

pedigree—a list of an animal's ancestors

register—to record a dog's breeding records with a kennel club

service dog—a dog trained to help a disabled person

sheepdog—a dog bred and used for herding sheep

signal dog—a dog trained to help people who cannot hear

veterinarian—a person trained and qualified to treat the diseases and injuries of animals

wean—to stop nursing or depending on a mother's milk

To Learn More

Alderton, David. *Dogs*. New York: Dorling Kindersley, 1993.

American Kennel Club. *The Complete Dog Book*. New York: Macmillan Publishing, 1992.

Emert, Phyllis Raybin. *Guide Dogs*. Mankato, Minn.: Crestwood House, 1985.

Ring, Elizabeth. *Assistance Dogs: In Special Service*. Brookfield, Conn.: The Millbrook Press, 1993.

Ring, Elizabeth. *Detector Dogs: Hot on the Scent*. Brookfield, Conn.: The Millbrook Press, 1993.

Rosen, Michael J. *Kids' Best Field Guide to Neighborhood Dogs*. New York: Workman, 1993.

You can read articles about German shepherds in *AKC Gazette*, *Dog Fancy*, and *Dog World* magazines.

Useful Addresses and Internet Sites

American Kennel Club
5580 Centerview Drive
Raleigh, NC 27606
E-mail address: info@akc.org
http://www.akc.org/akc/

Canadian Kennel Club
100–89 Skyway Avenue
Etobicoke, ON M9W 6R4
Canada

The Dog Museum
1721 South Mason Road
St. Louis, MO 63131

German Shepherd Dog Club of America
17 West Ivy Lane
Englewood, NJ 07631

North American Search Dog Network
Route 2, Box 32
Urbana, IL 61801

The Seeing Eye
P.O. Box 375
Morristown, NJ 07963

Therapy Dogs International
6 Hilltop Road
Mendham, NJ 07945

Cyber-Pet
http://www.cyberpet.com

Dog Owner's Guide
http://www.canismajor.com/dog/

German Shepherd Dog Home Page
http://www.sofcom.com.au/GSD/

Wunderhund!
http://www.pcnet.com/~dogginit/HOME.html

Index